Exploring
Mars

by Erin Rogers

Editorial Offices: Glenview, Illinois • Parsippany, New Jersey • New York, New York
Sales Offices: Needham, Massachusetts • Duluth, Georgia • Glenview, Illinois
Coppell, Texas • Ontario, California • Mesa, Arizona

Welcome to Mars: The Red Planet

Have you ever looked at the sky through a telescope? If you have, you may have noticed stars and the planets of our solar system illuminating, or lighting up, the night sky. One planet that is often visible from Earth is Mars. Mars is the fourth planet from the sun and the next planet beyond Earth. Even when it is closest to the sun, Mars is about 128 million miles away from it. When Mars comes closest to Earth, it is about 35 million miles away.

Mars is the third smallest planet in our solar system. It is about half the size of Earth. Because of its bloodlike color, Mars was given its name by the ancient Romans in honor of their god of war.

The Solar System

Our solar system is made up of the sun, the nine planets, asteroids, comets, and dust. The sun is in the center of the solar system. It is just one star out of billions in our universe. Stars are formed from clouds of gas, which **collapse** due to the force of gravity.

Each planet has a different orbit around the sun. The closest planet to the sun is Mercury. The farthest planet from the sun is Pluto. Look at the picture to see where Mars is in relation to the other eight planets in our solar system.

Our solar system is just one of many in our **galaxy.** A galaxy is a large system of stars and interstellar matter, which floats between the stars.

Our galaxy is called the Milky Way. The universe is made up of billions of galaxies. Each galaxy usually has between several million and several trillion stars.

Astronomers estimate that the Milky Way galaxy has several billion stars. The distance from one side of our galaxy to the opposite side is more than 100,000 light years. That means that it takes light 100,000 years to travel from one side to the other!

The nine planets of our solar system orbit the sun.

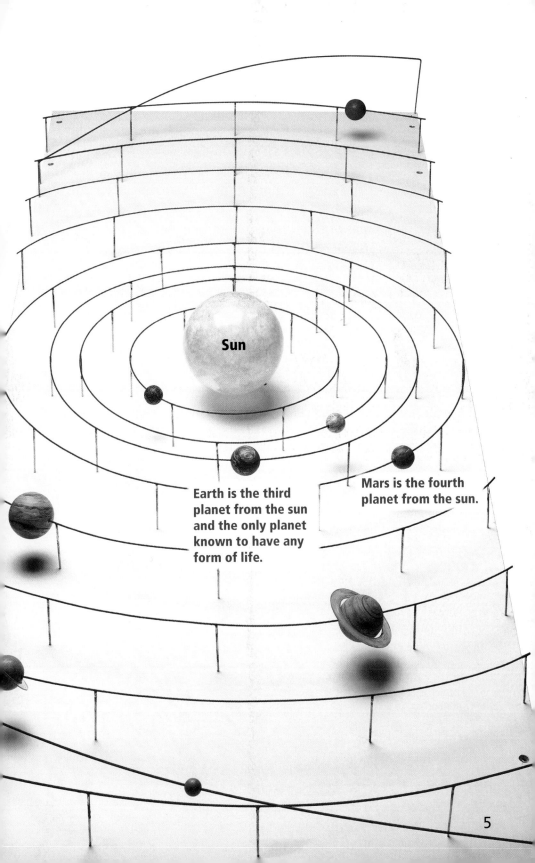

Sun

Earth is the third planet from the sun and the only planet known to have any form of life.

Mars is the fourth planet from the sun.

5

The Surface of Mars

Except for Earth, Mars has the most varied and interesting terrain of all the planets. The surface of Mars can be divided into three different regions: bright areas, dark areas, and polar caps.

The bright areas of Mars cover about two-thirds of its surface. These areas look like the deserts we have on Earth. Ferric oxide, or rusty iron, is present in the sandy soil. This gives the planet its reddish color.

The dark areas of Mars cover about one-third of the planet's surface. They are called the Maria, or seas of sand. The Maria change color depending on the season. During the Martian fall and winter, the Maria may become so light that they look as if they have disappeared. During the Martian spring and summer, these areas become a dark bluish-gray or greenish-gray color. Astronomers believe the changes in color are caused by strong winds that move the sand around. The sand covers and uncovers parts of the surface of Mars, causing it to change color.

The third region, the polar caps, can be found at the North and South Poles of the planet. These caps look white from Earth. Many scientists believe that the color comes from large amounts of water frozen there. They also contain solid carbon dioxide, or dry ice. The polar caps advance and retreat with the passing seasons. The summer can get warm enough to free some of the poles' frozen carbon dioxide. However, the water ice remains permanently frozen.

Like our South Pole , Mars's South Pole (background of page) is completely frozen and can be found at the southernmost point on the planet.

The polar caps (one of which is shown above) are located at the North and South Poles of Mars. They are made of ice and solid carbon dioxide. They change size depending on the season.

Besides these three regions, the surface of Mars has many craters. Craters form when meteors or meteorites **collide** with a planet. The impact of such a collision leaves a giant depression on the surface. Other features of Mars include canyons, gorges, and volcanoes. The largest volcano on Mars is more than twice the size of Mauna Loa, which is the highest volcano on Earth! Mars also has what scientists think are dry riverbeds. Many scientists believe Mars once had flowing water, and these dry riverbeds help support that hypothesis.

This crater is just one of many craters on the surface of Mars. Craters form when meteorites or other celestial bodies collide with the surface of the planet.

Life on Mars?

Conditions on Mars are more like the conditions on Earth than on any other planet scientists have found. Because Earth's conditions are suitable for some forms of life, scientists have often wondered whether there could be life on Mars too.

In 1877 an astronomer named Giovanni Schiaparelli noted that there are many lines that crisscross the dark area of Mars. They became known as canals. Many people began to believe that some sort of life form must have built these canals. However, in 1969 space probes *Mariner 6* and *Mariner 7* took pictures from several hundred miles above the surface of Mars. The pictures showed that the canals were naturally made canyons.

Scientists are still trying to find out whether there is or has ever been life on Mars. Scientist David McKay found possible evidence of life on a meteorite from Mars. He claims that air pockets on the meteorite could be the result of life forms such as bacteria. However, other scientists argue that the pockets could have been the result of changes in temperature.

Even so, more than three decades of missions to Mars have revealed much more about its surface. Some scientists believe that the system of giant canyons, called Valles Marineris, could be the result of erosion by rivers of water. The probability of the presence of water leads some scientists to think that Mars may have had some form of life a long time ago. This still has not been proven.

The Atmosphere of Mars

If the conditions on Mars are similar to the conditions we have on Earth, then could humans survive on Mars? Astronomers have found that this might be possible but very difficult, partly because of Mars's atmosphere.

Unlike Earth's atmosphere, the atmosphere on Mars is mostly made up of carbon dioxide. This is the substance that we breathe out of our lungs as waste. There are small amounts of other gases in the air of Mars, shown on the chart below.

Another major difference between the atmosphere of Earth and that of Mars is the atmospheric pressure. Atmospheric pressure is the force pushing on you from the tiny **particles** that make up air. The atmospheric pressure on Earth is about 14.7 pounds per square inch. The atmosphere on Earth is much more **compact** than the atmosphere on Mars. The atmospheric pressure on Mars is only one-tenth of a pound per square inch, which is less than one-hundredth the amount of pressure on Earth!

Contents of the Martian Atmosphere	
Carbon Dioxide	95.32%
Nitrogen	2.75%
Argon	1.6%
Oxygen	0.13%
Water	0.03%
Neon	0.00025%

Mars's sky has clouds just like Earth's sky does. There are three types of clouds on Mars: pink clouds, blue clouds, and white clouds. The pink clouds are made up of dust and are the most common. There are also blue clouds, which are made up of ice crystals. Scientists believe that the white clouds are made of water vapor, just like the clouds in Earth's atmosphere.

The temperatures on Mars are much colder than the temperatures on Earth. This is because Mars is farther away from the sun. The average temperature on Mars is $-62.8°C$ ($-81°F$). When it gets really cold, temperatures can get as low as $-140°C$ ($-220°F$). The coldest temperature recorded on Earth is $-88.9°C$ ($-128°F$), which was in Antarctica. However, there are times when the temperatures on Mars are about the same as the temperatures on Earth. Temperatures on Mars can get as high as $20°C$ ($68°F$). However, it is rarely warmer than $0°C$ ($32°F$).

Temperature on Mars in degrees Fahrenheit	
Average	−81
Minimum	−220
Maximum	68

Mars's pink clouds are made of dust and cover more area on that planet than any other type of cloud.

The Moons of Mars

From Earth, we can usually see our moon shining at night. If we lived on Mars, we would be able to see not one moon, but two in the sky! Mars has two moons that orbit close to its surface. The larger moon is named Phobos, and the smaller moon is Deimos. In Greek mythology, Phobos and Deimos are sons of Aries. Aries is the ancient Greek god of war, just as Mars is the Roman war god.

Deimos is the smallest moon in our solar system. It has a diameter of approximately eight miles. Although Phobos is the larger of the two moons, it is still one of the smallest in our solar system. Its diameter is approximately fourteen miles. Phobos orbits closer to the surface of Mars than Deimos. Both Phobos and Deimos are made of a combination of carbon-rich rock and ice.

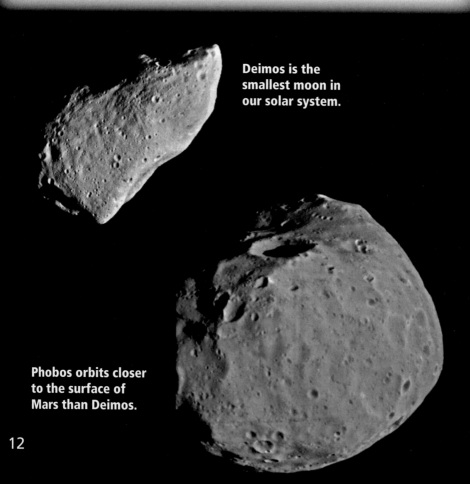

Deimos is the smallest moon in our solar system.

Phobos orbits closer to the surface of Mars than Deimos.

Missions to Mars

Because Mars is so close to Earth, it has been possible for us to send probes into space to find out more about our neighboring planet. So far, the exploration of Mars has occurred in three stages. In the first stage, when the United States was beginning to explore the solar system, the National Aeronautics and Space Administration (NASA) sent spacecraft to fly by Mars. These missions were called flyby missions. In a flyby mission, the spacecraft took as many pictures as possible of the planet as it passed by.

On November 28, 1964, NASA sent a spacecraft called *Mariner 4* into space. On July 14, 1965, *Mariner 4* passed by Mars and started taking close-range pictures of its surface. This was the first time a spacecraft had ever gotten so close to the planet. *Mariner 4* was only expected to survive for eight months, but it actually lasted about three years. The spacecraft continued sending data, and scientists were able to get measurements of Martian winds.

This spacecraft was designed to fly near Mars to take close-range pictures of its surface.

The second type of mission to Mars is called an orbiter mission. As space technology became more advanced, scientists began putting spacecraft in orbit around Mars. This allowed them to observe Mars for longer periods of time.

On May 30, 1971, NASA sent *Mariner 9* into space. It was the first artificial satellite of Mars. This means that it was the first human-made object to orbit Mars. The *Mariner 9* stayed in orbit around Mars for about a year. This spacecraft was very successful because it was able to map the whole surface of Mars. It was also the first to take close-up pictures of Phobos and Deimos. Two very important features were discovered during this mission: Olympus Mons, Mars's huge volcano, and Valles Marineris.

The third type of mission is called a lander mission. In these missions, spacecraft go to Mars and land on its surface. Today it is possible for a spacecraft to land on Mars and move around on its surface. This new technology allows scientists to get detailed information about Mars.

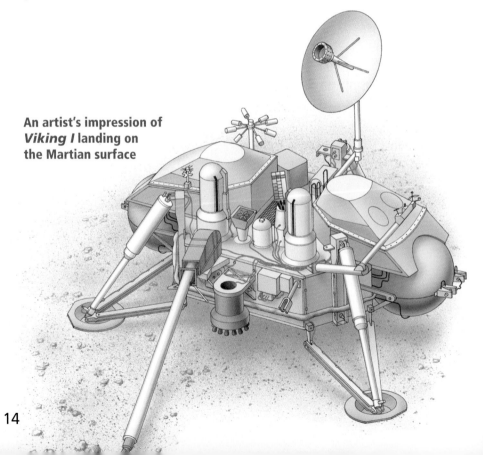

An artist's impression of *Viking I* landing on the Martian surface

On August 20, 1975, NASA sent the *Viking I* spacecraft into space. *Viking I* was both an orbiter and a lander. It first entered the orbit of Mars on June 19, 1976, and then it split into two separate pieces. One piece stayed in orbit around Mars, while the other floated down to land on the surface on July 20, 1976. This was the first time a spacecraft was able to land on the surface of another planet.

Shortly after launching *Viking I*, NASA sent *Viking II* into space. *Viking II* was identical to *Viking I*, but it landed on Mars in a different area, so more of the surface of the planet could be explored. *Viking II* arrived to orbit Mars on July 3, 1976. The lander started exploring the surface on August 7, 1976.

In 2004, NASA sent up twin landers *Spirit* and *Opportunity* to explore the red planet. Their job was to take soil samples and examine craters for evidence of water and dry lakes. Both of them sent back amazing images of the Martian landscape.

This spacecraft, called *Viking I*, was able to land on the surface of Mars, allowing scientists to explore the planet in a way they never could before.

The Seasons of Mars

Like Earth, Mars has seasons. They depend on where the planet is in relation to the sun. The reason that we have seasons on Earth is because of the tilt of Earth's rotational axis. Mars also has a tilt in its axis. For this reason it has seasons similar to Earth's. However, there is another factor in determining the seasons on Mars.

When Earth and Mars are in their orbits, they follow elliptical, or oval, paths around the sun. However, the orbit of Mars takes it much farther away from the sun than Earth's orbit. This affects the length of each season on Mars.

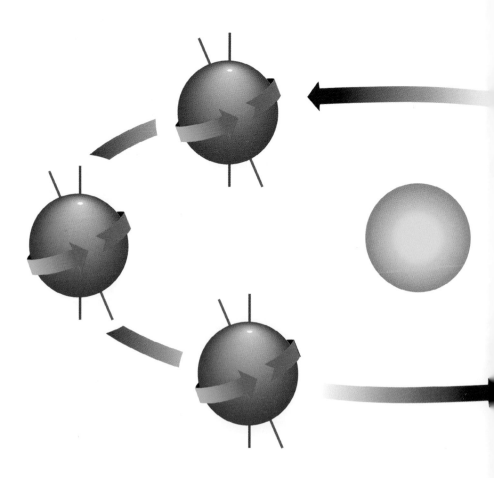

In a planet's orbit, the closest point to the sun is called *perihelion*, and the farthest point from the sun is called *aphelion*. You can see these two points in the diagram below. When Mars is closest to the sun in its orbit, it moves much faster than when it is farther away. This is because the force of gravity that holds Mars in its orbit around the sun is strongest when the planet is closest to the sun.

The seasons on Mars vary depending on the hemisphere. In the northern hemisphere of Mars, winter is short and relatively mild, while summer is long and cool. In the southern hemisphere, the summer is short and relatively warm, while winter is long and cold.

Because Earth is closer to the sun, Earth moves around the sun more quickly than Mars does. A Martian day takes 24 hours and 39 minutes. A Martian year takes 687 Earth days.

Every twenty-six months, Earth passes Mars in its orbit. Astronomers call this event an "opposition." During an opposition, the sun, Earth, and Mars form a straight line. Earth is always in the middle between the sun and Mars. At the time of an opposition, the distance between Mars and Earth is the shortest.

The rotational tilt of Mars is represented by the blue line. Earth's rotational axis is represented by the red line.

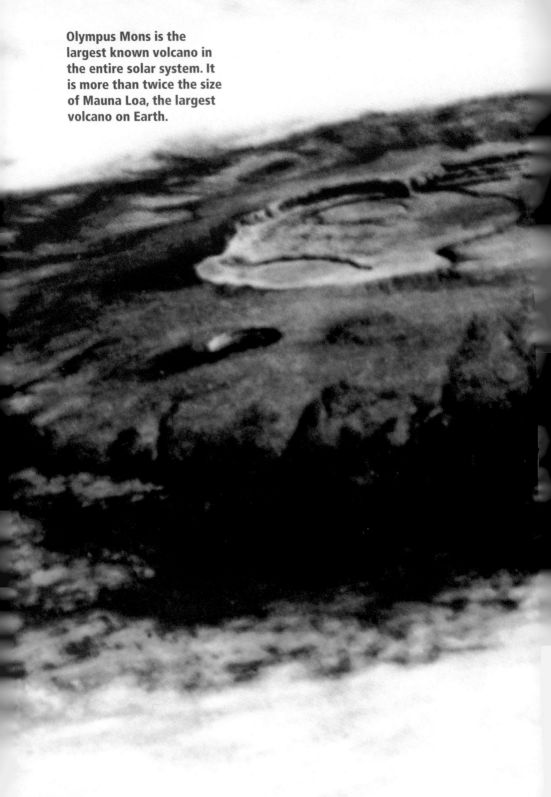

Olympus Mons is the largest known volcano in the entire solar system. It is more than twice the size of Mauna Loa, the largest volcano on Earth.

Landmarks on Mars

There are landmarks on Mars just as there are on Earth. For example, Mars is the home of the largest volcano in the entire solar system. This mountain is called Olympus Mons. Olympus Mons is almost thirteen miles high. Can you imagine climbing a mountain that high? The base of the mountain has a diameter of more than three hundred miles. If it were on Earth, it would cover the entire state of Arizona!

Olympus Mons can be found within another landmark on the surface of Mars. It is called Tharsis, and it is the largest volcanic region on the surface of the planet. Tharsis is about 2,400 miles across and 6.2 miles high.

Three other massive volcanoes are located in this region. They are called Ascraeus Mons, Pavonis Mons, and Arsia Mons. The volcanoes in the Tharsis region are much bigger than the volcanoes on Earth. The lava that flowed from these volcanoes is estimated to be 1 to 3 billion years old.

A third landmark on the surface of Mars is Hellas Planitia. This crater is about 4 miles deep and 1,250 miles wide. Scientists estimate that the crater was formed almost 4 billion years ago when an asteroid collided with the surface of the planet.

Craters are very common on the surface of Mars. However, there is another feature that scientist believe may have been created by water, rather than an asteroid. It is called Valles Marineris. Valles Marineris is a system of canyons about 2,500 miles long and from 1 to 4.5 miles deep. It is the largest and deepest known canyon in the solar system. This area is so big that if it were on Earth it would stretch all the way across the United States!

It is located just south of the Martian equator. Because the Valles Marineris canyons are so large, scientists have called this area the Grand Canyon of Mars. However, compared to Valles Marineris, the Grand Canyon is just a scratch on the surface of our planet!

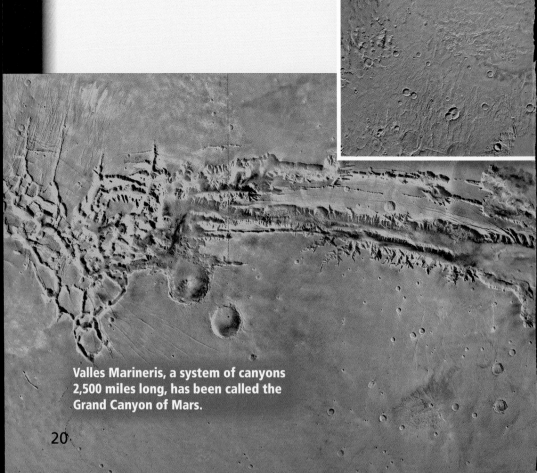

Valles Marineris, a system of canyons 2,500 miles long, has been called the Grand Canyon of Mars.

Martian Dust Storms

Mars is known to have dust storms so big that they cover the entire planet! This was discovered by one of the *Viking* missions. These global dust storms usually begin in the southern hemisphere of the planet. They typically start out small but grow into huge storms that spread out over vast regions of the planet. Martian dust storms tend to form in the spring and summer, although they do not occur every year. These dust storms erode the rocks on the surface of Mars.

This photograph shows Hellas Planitia, the largest crater on the surface of Mars.

The Future of Mars Exploration

What will the future hold for Mars exploration? NASA is already planning many new short-term expeditions to our neighboring red planet. Future missions will be able to take extreme close-up pictures of the surface of Mars. They will look for new landing sites that will be safe for future spacecraft, and they will continue the search for water under the surface of Mars.

NASA also has long-term plans for the exploration of Mars. Eventually, NASA hopes to achieve its first mission to bring Martian rocks and soil back to Earth. They also hope to develop the technology to send people to the surface of Mars. This will allow further investigation into the workings of the planet.

Now that you know about Mars, perhaps you are curious to see it for yourself. The best time to spot Mars is in the middle of the night. This is the time when Mars is highest in our sky. The higher Mars is in the sky, the clearer the planet will appear. Maybe one day, with new space technology, you will find yourself walking the red soil of planet Mars.

Scientists continue to create new tools to help them explore the surface of Mars.

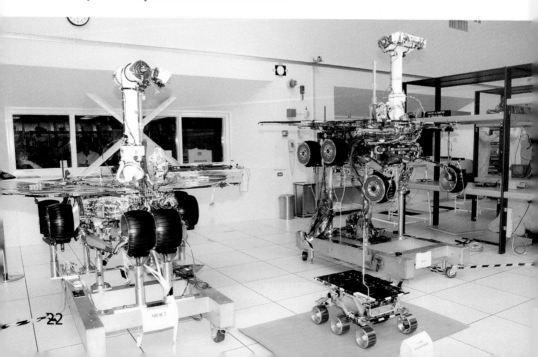

As technology advances, NASA scientists hope to send people to Mars. The top and left illustrations show what artists think it might be like to live and work on Mars.

Glossary

astronomers *n.* experts in astronomy, the science that deals with the sun, moon, planets, stars, etc.

collapse *v.* to shrink together suddenly; to curve in.

collide *v.* to hit or strike violently together; to crash.

compact *adj.* firmly packed together; closely joined.

galaxy *n.* a group of billions of stars forming one system.

particles *n.* very tiny bits of matter.